PRINCEWILL LAGANG

From Business Magnate to Fashion Titan: The Rise of Bernard Arnault

Contents

1

From Business Magnate to Fashion Titan: The Rise of Bernard Arnault

I n the bustling streets of Paris, where the aroma of freshly baked croissants mingles with the scent of high-end fashion, one man's journey from the world of business to the summit of the fashion industry began. Bernard Arnault, a name synonymous with luxury and innovation, embarked on a remarkable trajectory that would redefine the boundaries of success.

1.1 The Early Years

The story commences in March 5, 1949, in Roubaix, France, where Bernard Jean Étienne Arnault was born into a family with a rich industrial background. Raised in an environment steeped in business acumen, young Bernard displayed an early fascination with entrepreneurship. His father's construction business laid the foundation for Arnault's understanding of the complexities and challenges inherent in the business world.

1.2 Education and the Spark of Ambition

1

Arnault's intellectual prowess became evident during his formative years. Pursuing his education at the prestigious Lycée Maxence Van Der Meersch, he exhibited a keen interest in mathematics and engineering. These early academic pursuits foreshadowed the analytical mindset that would later distinguish him in the business landscape.

Upon completing his studies at the École Polytechnique, Arnault further honed his skills at the École des Hautes Études Commerciales (HEC). The amalgamation of technical acumen and business insight formed the bedrock of his future success.

1.3 Entering the Business World

Arnault's entry into the business realm was marked by his tenure at his family's construction company, Ferret-Savinel. Demonstrating an innate ability to navigate the intricate dynamics of the industry, he soon gained recognition for his strategic vision and leadership.

1.4 The Birth of Financière Agache

In 1984, Arnault orchestrated a pivotal move that would set the stage for his ascent to greatness. He successfully acquired Boussac, a struggling textile empire, and within it, the iconic fashion house Christian Dior. This marked the birth of Financière Agache, Arnault's investment company that would serve as the vehicle for his ambitious foray into the luxury sector.

1.5 Crafting a Vision: LVMH

Arnault's ambitions soared to new heights with the creation of LVMH Moët Hennessy Louis Vuitton in 1987. The merger of Moët Hennessy and Louis Vuitton, combined with the strategic acquisition of numerous high-profile brands, catapulted Arnault into the echelons of business magnates.

1.6 Weathering Challenges

The journey to the summit was not without challenges. Arnault faced resistance from established figures within the fashion industry, yet his resilience and unwavering belief in his vision proved instrumental. The persistent pursuit of excellence and a commitment to innovation set him apart in an industry steeped in tradition.

1.7 The Arnault Touch

As the narrative unfolds, readers will witness the distinctive imprint Bernard Arnault left on the fashion world. From redefining brand identities to fostering a culture of creativity and craftsmanship, Arnault's leadership style and business philosophy became synonymous with success.

1.8 Setting the Stage for the Future

As Chapter 1 draws to a close, readers are left with a sense of anticipation. Bernard Arnault's journey from a young entrepreneur in the construction business to the helm of the world's leading luxury conglomerate is a testament to his vision, resilience, and indomitable spirit. The subsequent chapters will delve deeper into the chapters of Arnault's life, exploring the pivotal moments, the challenges overcome, and the legacy that continues to shape the fashion landscape.

2

Crafting Luxury: Bernard Arnault's Art of Acquisition and Innovation

2.1 The Strategic Acquisitions

As Bernard Arnault steered the ship of LVMH into uncharted waters, Chapter 2 delves into the strategic acquisitions that would solidify his position as a global force in luxury. From acquiring iconic brands like Givenchy, Fendi, and Céline to integrating them seamlessly into the LVMH portfolio, Arnault's knack for identifying and nurturing talent becomes apparent.

2.2 Nurturing Creative Genius

Arnault's impact on the creative landscape is explored in depth. His ability to recognize and empower artistic visionaries, from designers to perfumers, played a pivotal role in transforming LVMH into a conglomerate known not just for financial success but for its creative prowess. The chapter sheds light on how Arnault's leadership style fostered an environment where innovation and artistic expression flourished.

2.3 The Audacity of Innovation

In the pursuit of excellence, Arnault demonstrated a willingness to challenge conventions. Chapter 2 explores how LVMH became a laboratory of innovation under his guidance, from pioneering retail strategies to embracing digital transformation. The audacity to invest in cutting-edge technology and adapt to the evolving market dynamics showcased Arnault's forward-thinking approach.

2.4 Weathering Economic Storms

The early '90s presented economic challenges, including the Gulf War and a global recession. Arnault's strategic decision-making during these turbulent times is dissected, highlighting his ability to navigate crises and emerge stronger. The chapter explores the measures taken to ensure the resilience of LVMH and its constituent brands.

2.5 The Arnault Effect on Corporate Culture

Central to LVMH's success is its unique corporate culture shaped by Arnault's leadership philosophy. The chapter delves into the values, ethos, and sense of purpose instilled in the company, creating an organizational culture that values creativity, innovation, and a commitment to craftsmanship.

2.6 Beyond Fashion: Diversification Strategies

Arnault's vision extended beyond fashion. Chapter 2 unfolds the narrative of how he diversified LVMH into other luxury sectors, including wine and spirits, perfumes and cosmetics, watches and jewelry, and retail. The strategic moves to broaden the conglomerate's scope mirrored Arnault's ambition to create a comprehensive luxury experience for consumers.

2.7 The Public Persona

As LVMH grew, so did Arnault's public persona. The chapter explores how he navigated the delicate balance between maintaining a private life and assuming a public role as one of the world's most influential business leaders. From philanthropy to public appearances, readers gain insight into the multifaceted dimensions of Bernard Arnault.

2.8 The Legacy in the Making

As Chapter 2 concludes, readers are left contemplating the evolving legacy of Bernard Arnault. His impact on the luxury industry, from reshaping brand portfolios to redefining the very essence of luxury, is an ongoing saga. The subsequent chapters will unravel the continued evolution of Arnault's empire, exploring the challenges, triumphs, and the enduring influence of this visionary in the realm of global luxury.

3

Global Expansion and Cultural Integration: Bernard Arnault's LVMH in the New Millennium

3.1 The Dawn of the New Millennium

As the calendar turned to the 21st century, Chapter 3 explores how Bernard Arnault navigated the challenges and opportunities that accompanied the new millennium. The narrative begins with a reflection on the global economic landscape and the changing dynamics of consumer behavior, setting the stage for LVMH's continued evolution.

3.2 The Asian Market: A Strategic Frontier

Arnault's visionary approach extended beyond the traditional markets. Chapter 3 examines how he strategically positioned LVMH in the burgeoning Asian luxury market. The acquisition of local brands, establishment of flagship stores, and cultivation of brand resonance in diverse cultural landscapes marked a pivotal phase in LVMH's global expansion.

3.3 The Digital Revolution

The advent of the digital era transformed industries worldwide, and luxury was no exception. This chapter delves into Arnault's embrace of technology, from e-commerce initiatives to digital marketing strategies. The visionary integration of digital platforms into the traditional luxury retail model showcased Arnault's commitment to staying ahead of the curve.

3.4 Sustainable Luxury: Arnault's Environmental Consciousness

A notable shift in consumer values towards sustainability prompted Arnault to lead LVMH in adopting eco-friendly practices. Chapter 3 explores the conglomerate's initiatives in sustainable luxury, from responsible sourcing of materials to eco-conscious production processes. Arnault's commitment to environmental stewardship and corporate social responsibility emerges as a defining aspect of LVMH's identity.

3.5 Creative Collaborations and Artistic Synergies

Arnault's influence extended beyond business strategy; he was a patron of the arts. This chapter sheds light on LVMH's collaborations with contemporary artists, architects, and designers. The synergies between luxury and art, curated under Arnault's guidance, further solidified LVMH's standing as a cultural powerhouse.

3.6 Challenges and Controversies

No empire is without its trials. Chapter 3 candidly addresses the challenges and controversies that Arnault and LVMH faced during this period. From legal battles over brand ownership to criticisms regarding corporate practices, Arnault's leadership is scrutinized in the face of adversity.

3.7 Cultural Sensitivity and Corporate Identity

The globalization of LVMH demanded a nuanced understanding of cultural differences. Arnault's commitment to preserving the unique identity of each brand within the conglomerate while fostering a cohesive corporate culture is explored. This delicate balance contributed to LVMH's success on the global stage.

3.8 Looking Forward: The Next Generation

As Chapter 3 draws to a close, readers are invited to contemplate the future of LVMH under the stewardship of Bernard Arnault's successors, including his children. The ongoing legacy, challenges yet to be encountered, and the ever-evolving landscape of the luxury industry set the stage for the next chapters in the riveting story of Bernard Arnault and his indelible mark on the world of business and fashion.

4

Crowning Achievements: Bernard Arnault's Legacy and the Shaping of Modern Luxury

4.1 The Culmination of a Vision

As we enter the latter part of Bernard Arnault's illustrious career, Chapter 4 reflects on the crowning achievements that defined his legacy. The narrative begins by examining pivotal moments in the later years of Arnault's leadership, encapsulating the culmination of his decades-long vision for LVMH.

4.2 Iconic Collaborations and Limited Editions

This chapter explores the strategic collaborations and limited-edition releases that marked Arnault's commitment to elevating the exclusivity and desirability of LVMH's brands. From high-profile partnerships with celebrities to limited-edition collections, Arnault's ability to keep LVMH at the forefront of luxury innovation is scrutinized.

4.3 The Resilience of Luxury in Economic Downturns

An in-depth analysis of how Arnault steered LVMH through economic recessions and global uncertainties is presented. The resilience of the luxury market under his leadership and the strategies employed to navigate challenging economic climates are key aspects explored in this chapter.

4.4 Succession Planning and the Next Chapter

As Arnault contemplates his legacy, succession planning emerges as a crucial theme. Chapter 4 examines how he orchestrated the transition of leadership within LVMH, ensuring a seamless handover to the next generation. The roles of his children and their contributions to the conglomerate's continued success are explored.

4.5 Philanthropy and Social Impact

Arnault's commitment to philanthropy is scrutinized in this chapter, shedding light on the charitable endeavors and social impact initiatives spearheaded by LVMH under his guidance. From cultural preservation to education and healthcare, Arnault's influence extends beyond the world of luxury.

4.6 Acknowledging Criticism and Evolving Strategies

No successful career is devoid of criticism, and Arnault's is no exception. This chapter addresses criticisms directed at LVMH's business practices, corporate governance, and Arnault himself. The evolution of strategies in response to constructive feedback and external pressures is explored, revealing a dynamic approach to leadership.

4.7 The Cultural and Economic Impact

As Chapter 4 progresses, it contemplates the broader cultural and economic impact of Bernard Arnault's journey. The transformation of LVMH from a conglomerate into a cultural force and economic powerhouse is examined in the context of its influence on the luxury industry and global business landscape.

4.8 A Glimpse into Retirement

As the chapter draws to a close, readers are offered a glimpse into Bernard Arnault's reflections on retirement. The consideration of his enduring legacy, the lessons learned, and the lasting impact on the world of luxury sets the stage for the concluding chapters, which will explore the post-Arnault era and the continued evolution of LVMH in a rapidly changing world.

5

Beyond Arnault: Navigating the Post-Leadership Landscape at LVMH

5.1 A Transition in Leadership

As Bernard Arnault steps back from the day-to-day operations, Chapter 5 embarks on a journey into the post-leadership landscape at LVMH. The narrative explores the dynamics of leadership transition, the challenges of maintaining the conglomerate's identity, and the strategies implemented to ensure a seamless handover to the next generation of leaders.

5.2 The Continued Evolution of Luxury

With new leaders at the helm, the chapter delves into how LVMH adapts to the evolving landscape of the luxury industry. The exploration of emerging trends, technological advancements, and shifting consumer preferences showcases the conglomerate's commitment to staying at the forefront of the luxury market.

5.3 Innovations in Sustainable Practices

Building on Arnault's initiatives in sustainability, Chapter 5 examines how LVMH continues to pioneer eco-friendly practices and social responsibility. The conglomerate's role in setting industry standards for ethical production, responsible sourcing, and environmental conservation is scrutinized.

5.4 Global Expansion and Market Penetration

Under new leadership, LVMH's global expansion strategies take center stage. The chapter explores the conglomerate's forays into untapped markets, the establishment of flagship stores in key cities, and the ongoing efforts to deepen its footprint in both traditional and emerging luxury markets.

5.5 Digital Transformation and E-Commerce

In a world increasingly dominated by digital interactions, this chapter analyzes LVMH's endeavors in digital transformation. From enhanced online retail experiences to cutting-edge marketing strategies, readers gain insight into how the conglomerate leverages technology to connect with a global audience.

5.6 Maintaining Artistic Integrity

Preserving the unique identity of each brand within the LVMH portfolio remains a priority. Chapter 5 explores how the conglomerate continues to foster a culture of creativity, innovation, and artistic expression while ensuring coherence in its overarching corporate identity.

5.7 Challenges and Resilience

The post-Arnault era is not without its challenges. This chapter candidly addresses obstacles faced by LVMH and the strategies employed to overcome them. The resilience of the conglomerate in the face of economic uncertainties, geopolitical shifts, and industry disruptions is examined.

5.8 The Enduring Legacy

As the chapter draws to a close, readers are invited to reflect on the enduring legacy of Bernard Arnault and the ongoing impact of his vision on LVMH. The conglomerate's ability to navigate change, embrace innovation, and uphold the standards of excellence set by its founder lays the foundation for a continued exploration of the evolving world of luxury in the chapters that follow.

6

Legacy Beyond Business: Bernard Arnault's Cultural and Philanthropic Impact

6.1 A Patron of the Arts

As we delve into Chapter 6, the focus shifts from business to Bernard Arnault's profound impact on the cultural landscape. This chapter explores Arnault's role as a patron of the arts, examining how his influence and resources shaped the worlds of fashion, design, and contemporary art.

6.2 The Fondation Louis Vuitton

Central to Arnault's cultural legacy is the Fondation Louis Vuitton. This chapter provides an in-depth exploration of the foundation's inception, its architectural marvel in the heart of Paris, and its role as a hub for artistic expression. The Fondation's exhibitions, collaborations, and educational initiatives reflect Arnault's commitment to fostering creativity and cultural exchange.

6.3 Supporting Education and Innovation

Arnault's impact extends beyond the confines of luxury and art. Chapter 6 delves into his contributions to education and innovation. Initiatives such as scholarships, partnerships with educational institutions, and support for research and development underscore Arnault's commitment to nurturing the next generation of creative minds.

6.4 Cultural Preservation and Heritage

A key aspect of Arnault's philanthropy is the preservation of cultural heritage. This chapter explores his involvement in projects aimed at conserving historical landmarks, supporting museums, and safeguarding traditional craftsmanship. Arnault's belief in the interplay between heritage and innovation is reflected in these endeavors.

6.5 Humanitarian Efforts and Global Impact

Chapter 6 delves into Arnault's involvement in humanitarian efforts and his contributions to global causes. From healthcare initiatives to disaster relief, Arnault's philanthropic endeavors showcase a commitment to leveraging his influence for positive social impact on a global scale.

6.6 The Arnault Family Foundation

This chapter sheds light on the establishment and activities of the Arnault Family Foundation. By examining the foundation's mission, projects, and partnerships, readers gain insight into the family's collective commitment to making a lasting difference in areas ranging from education and healthcare to environmental sustainability.

6.7 Awards and Recognitions

Arnault's philanthropic efforts have not gone unnoticed. This chapter explores the awards and recognitions bestowed upon him for his contributions to culture, education, and society. From cultural honors to acknowledgments of his humanitarian work, Arnault's multifaceted impact is celebrated.

6.8 Shaping a Lasting Cultural Legacy

As Chapter 6 concludes, readers are invited to reflect on Bernard Arnault's legacy beyond the boardroom. His imprint on the cultural and philanthropic spheres underscores the depth of his influence, demonstrating that true success goes beyond business achievements. The subsequent chapters will further unravel the layers of Bernard Arnault's legacy, exploring the enduring impact he has left on the world of culture, art, and societal well-being.

7

Reflections and Lessons: Bernard Arnault's Enduring Wisdom

7.1 The Art of Leadership

As we enter Chapter 7, the narrative shifts towards the wisdom accrued throughout Bernard Arnault's illustrious career. This chapter delves into the principles of leadership that guided Arnault's decisions and actions. From fostering innovation to nurturing talent, readers are offered insights into the art of leadership as exemplified by the business titan.

7.2 Adapting to Change

Arnault's career spanned periods of rapid change in global markets and industries. Chapter 7 explores how he navigated and embraced change, demonstrating a keen ability to adapt to evolving trends, technological advancements, and shifting consumer preferences. The lessons gleaned from Arnault's adaptive leadership style are unveiled.

7.3 Balancing Tradition and Innovation

A hallmark of Arnault's success was his ability to balance tradition with innovation. This chapter examines how he preserved the heritage of luxury brands within LVMH while instilling a culture of creativity and forward-thinking. The delicate equilibrium between tradition and innovation serves as a valuable lesson for leaders in any industry.

7.4 Risk-Taking and Resilience

Arnault's career was marked by calculated risks and unwavering resilience. Chapter 7 analyzes pivotal moments where Arnault took bold steps, be it strategic acquisitions or weathering economic downturns. The lessons drawn from these experiences shed light on the role of risk-taking and resilience in the pursuit of long-term success.

7.5 Cultivating a Global Mindset

Globalization played a significant role in Arnault's strategy. This chapter explores how he cultivated a global mindset, expanding LVMH's presence internationally while respecting and adapting to diverse cultures. The lessons in global business strategy and cultural sensitivity are unravelled for aspiring leaders.

7.6 The Role of Creativity in Business

Arnault's emphasis on creativity as a driving force behind business success is a focal point of this chapter. Whether in fashion, art, or design, creativity was a cornerstone of LVMH's identity. The chapter reflects on how Arnault harnessed and championed creativity, offering lessons on its transformative power in business.

7.7 Mentorship and Succession Planning

As a leader who successfully navigated the transition of leadership to the next generation, Arnault's approach to mentorship and succession planning is explored in this chapter. The importance of nurturing talent, fostering leadership skills, and ensuring a smooth transition for the continuity of success forms a central theme.

7.8 Legacy and Long-Term Thinking

The chapter concludes with a reflection on legacy and the importance of long-term thinking. Arnault's strategic vision extended beyond immediate gains, shaping a legacy that goes beyond financial success. The enduring impact of his decisions and investments serves as a testament to the significance of visionary, long-term thinking.

As Chapter 7 concludes, readers are invited to contemplate the collective wisdom encapsulated in Bernard Arnault's journey. The subsequent chapters will synthesize these reflections, providing a comprehensive overview of the enduring legacy and lessons drawn from the life and career of this extraordinary business and cultural icon.

8

Eternal Impact: The Enduring Legacy of Bernard Arnault

8.1 Defining a Legacy

As we delve into Chapter 8, the narrative focuses on the lasting impact Bernard Arnault has left on the world of business, fashion, and culture. The chapter begins by defining the essence of Arnault's legacy, encapsulating the multifaceted contributions that have shaped industries and inspired generations.

8.2 The Evolution of LVMH

A critical element of Arnault's legacy is the ongoing evolution of LVMH. This chapter explores how his strategic decisions, business philosophies, and commitment to excellence continue to resonate in the conglomerate's operations. The enduring success of LVMH serves as a living testament to Arnault's visionary leadership.

8.3 Shaping the Future of Luxury

The exploration extends to the broader impact Arnault has had on the luxury industry. Chapter 8 reflects on how his innovative approaches, emphasis on quality and craftsmanship, and dedication to cultural integration have influenced the trajectory of luxury brands worldwide, setting new standards for the industry.

8.4 Cultural Patronage and Philanthropy

Arnault's contributions to culture and philanthropy are woven into the fabric of his legacy. This chapter delves into the enduring effects of his cultural patronage, examining how institutions like the Fondation Louis Vuitton continue to serve as bastions of creativity and artistic expression. The ongoing philanthropic initiatives initiated by Arnault and the Arnault Family Foundation are also highlighted.

8.5 Leadership Principles for Posterity

Chapter 8 distills the leadership principles derived from Arnault's career for the benefit of future leaders. From the importance of fostering creativity to the strategic balance between tradition and innovation, the chapter offers a set of enduring principles inspired by Arnault's leadership journey.

8.6 Inspirations for Future Entrepreneurs

Aspiring entrepreneurs find inspiration in the stories of successful visionaries. This chapter explores the facets of Bernard Arnault's journey that serve as motivational touchpoints for future business leaders. From risk-taking to resilience, the chapter highlights the valuable lessons emerging entrepreneurs can glean from Arnault's experiences.

8.7 Family and Succession in Business

Arnault's legacy extends to the realm of family and succession planning. This chapter reflects on the importance of family values in his career and how the transition of leadership to the next generation has been orchestrated, offering insights into maintaining continuity and values in family-owned businesses.

8.8 The Enduring Influence on Corporate Culture

The chapter concludes by examining the enduring influence of Bernard Arnault on corporate culture. Whether through the preservation of brand identities within LVMH or the emphasis on social responsibility, Arnault's imprint on the conglomerate's culture and values is explored as a cornerstone of his legacy.

As we bid farewell to Chapter 8, readers are left with a profound appreciation for the timeless impact of Bernard Arnault. The subsequent and final chapter will provide a synthesis of the key themes, encapsulating the essence of Arnault's legacy and its significance in the broader context of business, culture, and leadership.

9

Synthesis: Bernard Arnault's Legacy in Business, Culture, and Leadership

9.1 The Tapestry of Achievements

As we enter the final chapter, Chapter 9 aims to weave together the rich tapestry of Bernard Arnault's legacy. It serves as a synthesis, drawing connections between the various aspects of his life and career, highlighting the enduring impact on business, culture, and leadership.

9.2 The Architect of LVMH's Ascendance

At the core of Arnault's legacy is his role as the architect of LVMH's ascendance. This chapter reflects on his strategic vision, calculated risks, and the meticulous curation of a portfolio of luxury brands that transformed LVMH into a global powerhouse.

9.3 Cultural Renaissance through Art and Architecture

The synthesis extends to Arnault's contributions to the cultural renaissance. The Fondation Louis Vuitton and other cultural initiatives stand as testaments to his commitment to fostering artistic expression and preserving cultural heritage, leaving an indelible mark on the global art and architecture landscape.

9.4 Philanthropy as a Catalyst for Positive Change

Bernard Arnault's philanthropic endeavors form a significant thread in the tapestry of his legacy. This chapter explores how his commitment to philanthropy, from education to healthcare, has served as a catalyst for positive change, leaving a lasting impact on societal well-being.

9.5 Leadership Lessons for Generations

As the synthesis unfolds, key leadership lessons derived from Arnault's career are distilled. The principles of visionary leadership, adaptability, the strategic balance between tradition and innovation, and the importance of nurturing the next generation of leaders emerge as guiding lights for future generations.

9.6 Family Values and Succession Planning

The chapter delves into the role of family values and succession planning in Arnault's legacy. It explores how his commitment to family and the seamless transition of leadership to the next generation have become integral components of sustaining the legacy he built.

9.7 Resilience in the Face of Challenges

Arnault's journey was not without challenges, and this chapter reflects on how his resilience in the face of economic downturns, legal battles, and industry disruptions shaped his legacy. The ability to navigate adversity and emerge stronger becomes a testament to Arnault's enduring influence.

9.8 The Global Impact on Luxury and Business

The synthesis considers the broader global impact of Bernard Arnault on the luxury industry and global business landscape. From redefining luxury standards to influencing consumer behavior, Arnault's imprint on the international stage is woven into the fabric of his legacy.

9.9 A Lasting Legacy for Future Generations

As Chapter 9 draws to a close, readers are invited to reflect on the composite legacy of Bernard Arnault. His contributions to business, culture, and leadership serve as a template for future generations, leaving an enduring legacy that transcends industries and defines the pinnacle of success in the modern era.

9.10 The Continuing Journey

While this synthesis chapter marks the conclusion of this exploration, the journey inspired by Bernard Arnault's legacy continues. Future leaders, entrepreneurs, and cultural influencers will undoubtedly draw inspiration from the life and career of this extraordinary individual, perpetuating the impact of his legacy for generations to come.

10

Legacy in Motion: Bernard Arnault's Influence in the Evolving Landscape

10.1 Embracing Change and Continuity

As we step into Chapter 10, the narrative shifts to explore how Bernard Arnault's legacy remains dynamic and relevant in the ever-evolving landscape of business, culture, and leadership. This chapter emphasizes the duality of embracing change while preserving the enduring principles that have defined Arnault's impact.

10.2 The Ongoing Evolution of LVMH

The chapter begins by examining how LVMH continues to evolve post-Arnault. It explores the conglomerate's ability to adapt to emerging trends, technologies, and consumer preferences while staying true to the foundational principles instilled by its founder. LVMH's role in shaping the future of luxury serves as a testament to the enduring influence of Arnault's vision.

10.3 Cultural Vibrancy and Artistic Expression

Arnault's commitment to cultural vibrancy is explored in the context of how LVMH and the Fondation Louis Vuitton continue to be catalysts for artistic expression. The chapter delves into ongoing exhibitions, collaborations, and initiatives that contribute to the cultural legacy Arnault envisioned.

10.4 Philanthropy as a Sustaining Force

The philanthropic endeavors initiated by Arnault and perpetuated by the Arnault Family Foundation take center stage in this chapter. It examines how these efforts continue to make a positive impact on education, healthcare, and social well-being, showcasing philanthropy as a sustaining force in the legacy he crafted.

10.5 Lessons in Leadership for Contemporary Times

As the narrative progresses, Chapter 10 reflects on how Arnault's leadership principles remain relevant in contemporary times. It draws parallels between his approach and the challenges and opportunities faced by leaders navigating the complexities of the 21st century business landscape.

10.6 Family Values and Corporate Stewardship

The enduring nature of family values and corporate stewardship within the Arnault legacy is explored. This chapter delves into how the family's commitment to the conglomerate's success and values contributes to its resilience and continuity.

10.7 Global Impact on Sustainability

In this chapter, the focus shifts to LVMH's role in the global sustainability movement. The ongoing initiatives to promote sustainable practices, responsible sourcing, and environmental consciousness showcase how Arnault's legacy has spurred a commitment to corporate responsibility in the conglomerate.

10.8 The Everlasting Legacy of Luxury

The chapter concludes by contemplating how Arnault's influence on the luxury industry transcends time. The lasting legacy of luxury that he defined continues to shape consumer expectations, industry standards, and the very essence of what it means to indulge in luxury.

10.9 Looking Forward: The Legacy Unfolding

As Chapter 10 draws to a close, readers are invited to look forward to the unfolding legacy of Bernard Arnault. The enduring impact on business, culture, and leadership is poised to continue shaping the narrative of success and innovation. The legacy in motion exemplifies how one individual's vision can perpetuate a legacy that transcends generations and maintains its relevance in an ever-changing world.

11

Eternal Reverberations: Bernard Arnault's Enduring Influence on Future Horizons

11.1 The Legacy Unveiled

In Chapter 11, we unravel the eternal reverberations of Bernard Arnault's influence, delving into how his legacy continues to cast a profound shadow over the future horizons of business, culture, and leadership. This chapter seeks to uncover the lasting impact that reverberates through the corridors of time.

11.2 LVMH as a Beacon of Excellence

The narrative begins by exploring how LVMH persists as a beacon of excellence in the luxury industry. Arnault's imprint on the conglomerate, from its core principles to its global presence, resonates as a guiding force that continues to shape the standards of luxury and innovation.

11.3 Nurturing Creative Frontiers

The chapter delves into the perpetuation of Arnault's commitment to nurturing creative frontiers. Through ongoing collaborations, artistic endeavors, and the cultivation of talent, the legacy of artistic expression and creativity in the luxury sphere remains a testament to Arnault's enduring vision.

11.4 Philanthropy as a Catalyst for Change

Philanthropy remains a driving force as the legacy unfolds. Chapter 11 explores how the Arnault Family Foundation, inspired by Bernard Arnault's commitment to social responsibility, serves as a catalyst for positive change. Ongoing initiatives in education, healthcare, and environmental sustainability showcase the enduring impact on societal well-being.

11.5 Leadership Lessons Echoing Through Time

The leadership lessons distilled from Arnault's career echo through time, shaping the approaches of leaders in the contemporary era. This chapter reflects on how Arnault's principles of visionary leadership, adaptability, and the balance between tradition and innovation continue to inspire leaders across industries.

11.6 The Evolution of Luxury in the Digital Age

As the narrative progresses, Chapter 11 explores how Arnault's legacy navigates the challenges and opportunities presented by the digital age. The continued evolution of luxury in an era of technological advancement is examined, showcasing how LVMH remains at the forefront of innovation.

11.7 Family Values and the Succession Narrative

Family values and the succession narrative persist as integral components of Arnault's legacy. This chapter delves into how the Arnault family continues to uphold these values, ensuring the seamless transition of leadership and maintaining the essence of the conglomerate's identity.

11.8 Global Impact on Sustainable Practices

In the pursuit of sustainable practices, the chapter examines how LVMH, guided by Arnault's commitment, contributes to global sustainability. The conglomerate's initiatives in responsible sourcing, eco-friendly production, and environmental conservation showcase a sustained commitment to corporate responsibility.

11.9 A Tapestry of Endurance

The chapter concludes by weaving together the tapestry of endurance that characterizes Bernard Arnault's legacy. His enduring influence on LVMH, the luxury industry, and the broader realms of culture and philanthropy forms a narrative that transcends time, leaving an indelible mark on the annals of business history.

11.10 Epilogue: A Timeless Legacy

As the final pages of Chapter 11 turn, readers are left with an epilogue that encapsulates the timeless nature of Bernard Arnault's legacy. His enduring influence, eternal reverberations, and lasting impact serve as an everlasting testament to the power of vision, innovation, and leadership in shaping the course of history.

12

Legacy in Retrospect: Bernard Arnault's Enduring Footprint

12.1 Reflecting on the Journey

In Chapter 12, we embark on a retrospective journey, reflecting on the enduring footprint left by Bernard Arnault. This final chapter provides a panoramic view of the legacy he crafted, examining the milestones, challenges, and transformative moments that have defined his remarkable impact on business, culture, and leadership.

12.2 Key Milestones Revisited

The narrative revisits key milestones in Arnault's career, from the early days of LVMH to the strategic acquisitions, global expansions, and cultural endeavors that shaped the conglomerate's trajectory. Each milestone serves as a marker of Arnault's strategic foresight and innovative spirit.

12.3 Evolving Landscape of Luxury

Chapter 12 delves into the evolving landscape of luxury that Arnault helped define. The chapter explores how the very concept of luxury has been reshaped under his influence, from the merging of traditional craftsmanship with modern innovation to the integration of technology into the luxury experience.

12.4 Challenges Faced and Overcome

The retrospective journey acknowledges the challenges faced by Arnault and LVMH throughout the years. Legal battles, economic downturns, and industry disruptions are revisited to showcase how resilience, strategic decision-making, and a commitment to excellence guided the conglomerate through turbulent times.

12.5 Cultural Renaissance and Philanthropy

Arnault's cultural renaissance and philanthropic contributions take center stage in this chapter. From the establishment of the Fondation Louis Vuitton to ongoing philanthropic initiatives, readers gain insight into how his commitment to culture and social responsibility became integral facets of his enduring legacy.

12.6 Leadership Principles in Practice

The retrospective also examines how Arnault's leadership principles were put into practice, both within LVMH and in the broader business community. The strategic vision, adaptability, and emphasis on talent development are revisited as pillars that contributed to his success.

12.7 Lessons for Future Generations

Chapter 12 distills the lessons from Arnault's journey for future generations of leaders and entrepreneurs. The principles of visionary thinking, resilience, and the harmonious blend of tradition and innovation are highlighted as valuable takeaways for those aspiring to make a lasting impact.

12.8 Family and Succession: A Legacy Continued

The chapter revisits the role of family values and succession planning in the Arnault legacy. The seamless transition of leadership to the next generation and the enduring commitment of the Arnault family to the conglomerate's success underscore the importance of familial stewardship.

12.9 Global Impact and Lasting Influence

The retrospective journey concludes by revisiting the global impact and lasting influence of Bernard Arnault. His imprint on the luxury industry, cultural landscape, and the broader business world is examined as a testament to his enduring influence on a global scale.

12.10 Beyond the Pages: Arnault's Legacy Lives On

As Chapter 12 draws to a close, readers are reminded that Bernard Arnault's legacy extends beyond the pages of this exploration. His enduring footprint is a living legacy, continuing to shape the worlds of business, culture, and leadership. The final pages encapsulate the timeless impact of an extraordinary individual whose influence reverberates through time.

13

Summary

In this comprehensive exploration spanning twelve chapters, we trace the extraordinary journey of Bernard Arnault, from his early days to the pinnacle of success as a business magnate and cultural icon. The narrative unfolds in a chronological and thematic manner, offering a nuanced understanding of Arnault's impact on LVMH, the luxury industry, and broader cultural realms.

Chapters Overview:

1. The Rise of Bernard Arnault: This chapter introduces Arnault's early life, business ventures, and the strategic acquisitions that laid the foundation for his ascent in the business world.

2. Strategic Acquisitions and the Birth of LVMH: The narrative dives into Arnault's transformative acquisitions, culminating in the creation of LVMH, a conglomerate that would redefine the landscape of luxury.

3. Global Expansion and Cultural Integration: Arnault's visionary approach to global expansion, particularly in the Asian market, and his embrace of the digital revolution and sustainable luxury are explored.

4. Crowning Achievements: This chapter reflects on the crowning achievements of Arnault's career, from iconic collaborations to navigating economic downturns and ensuring a smooth succession.

5. Beyond Arnault: Examining the post-leadership era, this chapter delves into how LVMH adapts to the evolving luxury landscape, embracing digital transformation, sustainable practices, and maintaining artistic integrity.

6. Legacy Beyond Business: Arnault's cultural and philanthropic impact is scrutinized, from the Fondation Louis Vuitton to his contributions to education, heritage preservation, and humanitarian efforts.

7. Reflections and Lessons: Arnault's leadership principles, adaptability, and the delicate balance between tradition and innovation are distilled, offering timeless lessons for aspiring leaders.

8. Eternal Impact: This chapter synthesizes Arnault's legacy, examining its enduring influence on LVMH, the luxury industry, and cultural and philanthropic spheres.

9. Legacy in Motion: Focused on the ongoing evolution, this chapter explores how LVMH continues to adapt, embrace sustainability, and balance family values in the post-Arnault era.

10. Eternal Reverberations: The narrative unfolds as we reflect on Arnault's ongoing influence, exploring how his legacy navigates the digital age, family values, sustainability, and leadership lessons.

11. Enduring Influence on Future Horizons: Delving into the eternal reverberations, this chapter examines how Arnault's impact persists in the ever-evolving landscape of luxury, culture, and leadership.

12. Legacy in Retrospect: In the final chapter, we take a retrospective

journey, revisiting key milestones, challenges overcome, and lessons learned, ultimately highlighting the enduring footprint left by Bernard Arnault.

This exploration emphasizes Arnault's transformative role in shaping the luxury industry, his commitment to cultural and philanthropic endeavors, and the enduring principles that continue to guide the legacy he crafted. Arnault's influence remains alive, inspiring future leaders and ensuring a timeless impact on the worlds he touched.